OUR DADDY IS
INVINCIBLE!

Written by Shannon Maxwell

Illustrated by Liza Biggers

FOREWORD BY ALEXIS MAXWELL

Dedication

ISBN 978-1-61751-003-8

Text copyright© 2010 by Shannon Maxwell
Illustrations copyright© 2010 by Liza Biggers.
All rights reserved.

Published by 4th Division Press

LCCN: 2010915414

Printed in South Korea on acid-free paper.

First Printing, 2010

This book is dedicated to my children, Alexis, Eric, and Cassidy, and all those children of wounded or disabled parents who constantly bring joy and energy to the household and help in the healing process.

Thank you for your laughter, for pitching in around the house, for filling in for mom and dad when you've been called to and, most of all, for your unconditional love!

Believe that time heals wounds.
Find **hope** in the newness and possibilities each day brings.
Seize new adventures and activities with your mom or dad.
Always **remember** to enjoy being a child.
Know that the love you share is the strongest weapon against all hurt and the brightest beam of light to guide you to new levels of happiness.

In honor of LtCol. Tim A. Maxwell, USMC (ret).
In memory of Army Spc. Ethan Biggers, age 22.

Alexis' Foreword

As a child, growing up, I always thought of my daddy as a superhero. This helped me when he was deployed overseas and went away on trips, because I thought he was invincible and could never get hurt. When he came home wounded, I was ten and a little confused. "How could my invincible daddy be hurt?"

As I learned more and finally saw him, I realized that the best part of him was there – his love for me. Even if the bad guys got him, he was still my daddy—a little different, but my wonderful father who loves me. My superhero would heal. Superman is hurt by Kryptonite, but he gets better and beats more bad guys. Same for daddies and mommies! You should always be proud of your parents because even if they had to leave you for a while and got hurt, they did it to protect you

and your family. They risked their lives for you and for others who needed help, like Superman does for the people of Metropolis. Your parents are strong and brave and can make it through anything—and so can you!

I'm now sixteen and each day my daddy and I are able to enjoy life together more and more, despite his injuries. He comes to my soccer games and helps me practice. We go to the beach, watch movies, play video games, and cook together. We can't play all the same games we used to, but we've found some new ones and continue to have fun. Some things have had to change, but it doesn't have to be all bad. Different can be good, too!

I hope you enjoy our story and Mrs. Biggers' beautiful illustrations. You, too, can find joy with your daddy and mommy.

My brother, Eric, and I believe our daddy is Superman!
He is smart and strong and always protects us and others.

He sometimes goes on long trips for work—
places we have not been and cannot imagine.

It can be scary to think of Daddy so far from home.
But we shoo those worries away, agreeing that nothing can hurt him.

6

"I'm too mean!" Daddy always says, making a scrunchy face.
No you're not, Daddy. Not to us.

We say our goodbyes and tell him to be safe.
Then we're off to find fun; there is school the next day.

Each night we ask for his protection.
Mommy tells us he's well and that he loves us very much.

Imagine how surprised we were when one day Mommy said,
"Daddy's been hurt, but it will all be okay".

Daddies can be hurt, you say.
How can that be? We didn't think it that way.

After all...

Our daddy is invincible!
He has the strength and power of a superhero!

At least that's what we thought...
But, now we know that things can happen even to daddies and mommies.

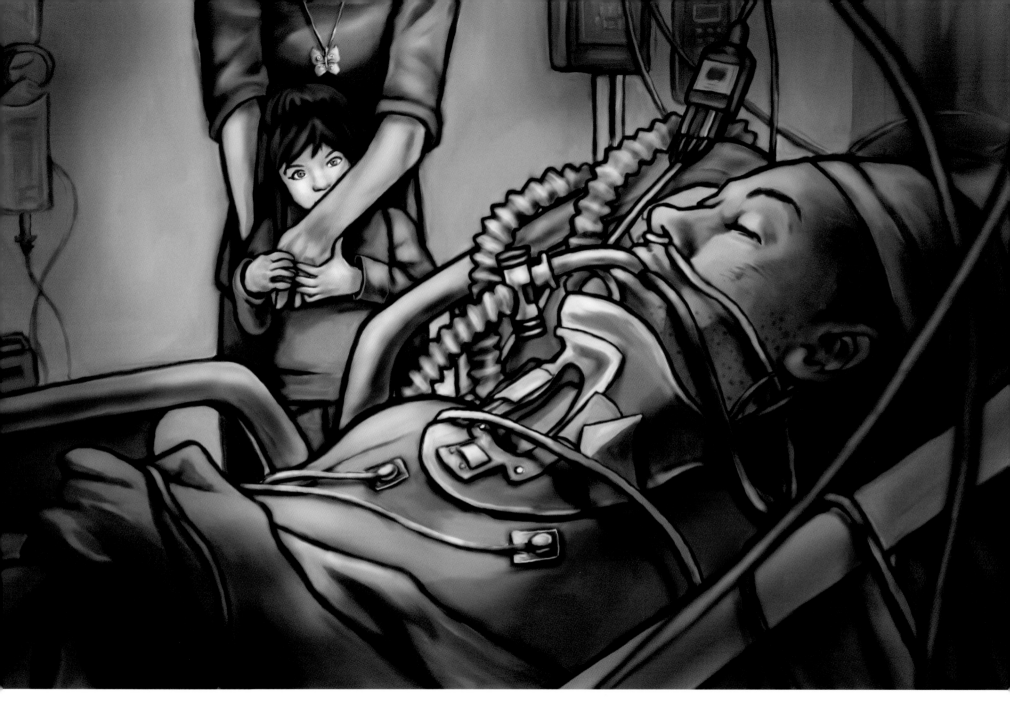

They sometimes get hurt, just like you and me.
Even superheroes get hurt by the villain sometimes.

It doesn't make them weaker, though.
Their injuries can't break their love for us or their inner strength and spirit

It takes a lot of courage and hard work to get better.
Every day our daddy trains his body and his mind, mending what was broken.

Some days are hard on the whole family.
Tears, yelling, and even his silence can make us feel like Daddy's upset with us.

But, we've come to realize he's frustrated with things he can't change now. We play quietly and after some time, daddy is back with hugs.

He exercises, eats healthy food, and gets lots of sleep—
things you and I do every day, too, as we grow bigger.

Even though he may be a little different now,
and can't do all the things we used to do, we still have fun.

He teaches us new games and we can teach him, too!
We laugh at old jokes and have come up with some new ones.

Our daddy is the bravest man we know.
We are so glad that he's here to see us grow.

So, take it from us,
my brother and me:

If this ever happens to you...
if your mommy or daddy gets hurt...

know there is a team of people who will help:
doctors, nurses, and therapists, too.

They work with mommies and daddies to help them heal—
in offices, hospitals, and at home.

With new legs, a wheel chair, a helmet, or cane,
they can do most anything.

Eric and I learned—and you will too—
our lives have not stopped because of our daddy's injuries.

Some changes will happen; that's only normal.
But, together you'll find new adventures and ways to make life wonderful!

Children just like you share their experiences of life with their parent or loved one after a traumatic injury. . .

"*My daddy takes me swimming; we walk our dog, Bella; and I sit in his chair and read to him. We also paint Easter eggs together.*"—Cassidy, age 8 (Adopted four years after her dad sustained a traumatic brain injury.) Montclair, VA

"*My daddy plays with me a lot, but I have to be careful with his arm. He watches cartoons with me, too. Daddy takes me to breakfast at Golden Corral sometimes on a date. I like when he does that. He can't throw me up anymore, but that is okay 'cause I am a big girl now. I feel bad for Daddy because his arm hurts a lot. I like to do dishes with Daddy now that I'm a big girl.*"—Karleigh, age 6 (Age 2 when her dad was injured in Iraq, suffering Traumatic Brain Injury (TBI), Post Traumatic Stress Syndrome (PTSD), nerve damage, and permanent deafness in his right ear.) Jacksonville, NC

"*When my dad got hurt it was scary and I was sad. But, I tried to cheer up because if he saw me sad then he would get sad. He worked hard to get better. After a while I realized my dad wasn't made worse by this. In fact, we still could do a lot together. We built a fort together and made a skateboard ramp and book shelves. Now, he comes to all my games too!*"—Eric, age 13 (Age 7 when his dad was wounded with a traumatic brain injury.) Montclair, VA

"Even though my dad is in a wheelchair, we still have a lot of fun. We go fishing, ride four-wheelers, play catch, and do a lot of things people that are not injured do." —Brandon, age 12 (Age 8 when his dad sustained a spinal cord injury and became a double amputee.) Richlands, NC

"We do a lot of things with our dad even though he cannot walk. We enjoy racing nitro cars, swimming, fishing, going to church, and many other activities. I am thankful that the Lord brought my dad home so that he can finish raising us and spend time with all of us." —Carl V, age 14 (Age 10 when his dad sustained a spinal cord injury and became a double amputee.) Richlands, NC

"My dad and I like to hang out! We do fun things like watch movies, go swimming, play games, ride bikes, [and] play dolls. I even get to sit on his lap when we go shopping." —Gracie, age 5 1/2 (Age 9 1/2 months when her dad was wounded and suffered an anoxic brain injury.) New Bern, NC

"This is my brother, Adam, and I am his little sister. Not much has changed, but you can still tell something is gone. We love to do all the things we did before the blast happened. Our favorite is going to Chucky Cheese before every deployment and we still go. I love my brother, Adam, and I know he still loves me." —Celine, age 12 (Age 7 when her brother sustained traumatic brain injury, severe hand damage, and post traumatic stress disorder due to Rocket Propelled Grenade (RPG) blast.) Tampa, FL

I was 11 when my dad was injured and my life was totally changed. When I heard that my dad had been hurt, I was very scared for him but also wondered if he would ever be the same again. Would he ever be able to play soccer with me? Chase me around the yard? Or even walk again? I just started praying. Two days later we heard that he was on his way to Walter Reed Hospital, so we immediately met him there. At first, I did not recognize him; almost every patient we saw on the way to see him was missing body parts. I had to take a double look at him. But I was proud of my dad for what he had done for our freedom. The first year was probably the hardest; after that [my] parents got divorced. When I realized that my dad was gonna be okay, I was relieved. My dad can do basically anything at this point, run, [be a] ski-instructor, sky dive, scuba dive, even climb mountains. But he also has Post Traumatic Stress Disorder (PTSD). My dad is a hero and my dad is a jerk. He would get upset over the smallest things, and he would treat my sister and I like soldiers. Eventually, after therapy and talking to the doctors, he has overcome it to where it isn't as bad. Today, my dad lives a normal life. He is re-married and loves life. If you did not know he was an amputee, you could not tell if he was wearing long pants. Thanks to all the troops and their families and the sacrifices they continue to make!

—Ethan, age 17
Havelock, NC

"My daddy looks different but he's the same as other daddies. It was sad when he had to go to the doctor because he had to have surgeries that hurt him. But, the doctors gave him medicine to help him feel better so that he didn't feel it. I really like to play with my daddy. He teaches me all kinds of sports so that I can play them! I like when my daddy and I do special things together. I would tell other kids that my daddy is just like their daddies. I'm proud of my daddy for being a brave Marine and never giving up."
—Trey, age 5 (Age 19 months when his dad was wounded in Iraq, sustaining third-degree burns over 50 percent of his body, a mild traumatic brain injury, inhalation injury, and a compressed fracture in his T-8 vertebrae.) Houston, TX

The butterfly is a symbol of HOPE.

Throughout the story there are butterflies—some hidden, some not.

Look and see if you can find them all.

Clues to where the butterflies are: p.4 girl's necklace, p.5 mom's mug and on counter, p.6 over trampoline, p.7 bath towel, p.8 garden ornament by house, p.9 nightstand, p.10 coloring book, p.11 flying to the right of boy, p.12 flying across page, p.13 dad's shoulder, p.14 yellow toy, p.15 mom's necklace, p.16 get well card on wall, p.17 little girl's purse, p.18 pencil mug, p.19 girl's bracelet, p.20 cup with straw, p.21 girl's bathing suit, p.22 girl's necklace and in grass, p.23 right side of soccer field, p.24 flying to the right of boy, p.25 flying right and left of kid's/girl's shirt, p.26 Speech Therapist's word card, p.27 blue shirt, p.28 girl's ski jacket, p.29 sitting on watch, p.30 kite.)

About the Author

Shannon Maxwell grew up in Texas and married her love, a Marine, LtCol. Tim Maxwell (ret), following him around the country as he served. In October 2004, her husband was wounded in Iraq with a severe traumatic brain injury. Inspired by his resilience throughout recovery and the indomitable spirit he shared with others, she and the family became advocates for the wounded and their families. Shannon co-founded the highly reputed non-profit/organizations, Hope For The Warriors® and SEMPERMAX *Support Fund*. She received the President's Volunteer Service Award from President George W. Bush and the National Military Family Association's VIP Award. She currently resides and works in Northern Virginia with her husband and three children, who are her daily inspiration to make a difference in the lives of others.

About the Illustrator

Liza Biggers is a freelance artist who grew up in Florida and spent her teen years in Ohio. She now lives in New York where she and her husband enjoy city life. Along with life experiences, her love of comics has been one of the largest influences on her art. In March 2006, Liza's brother, Ethan, was shot by a sniper in Baghdad and succumbed to his wounds in February 2007 after a long battle. Liza never left his side and served as one of his primary caregivers. Her illustrations in this book are works of love, dedicated to Ethan's memory and his service for others. www.lizabiggers.com

To the Adults . . .

I began writing *Our Daddy Is Invincible!* when sitting in Bethesda National Naval Medical Center's ICU waiting room after my husband, Tim, was wounded. A few days prior, in order to be at Tim's bedside in Germany, I had left my children, Alexis and Eric, then 10 and 7 respectively, at our North Carolina home in the care of my sister, Sandra, and her husband, Rick. Telling the children that their father had been wounded was hard. Leaving them so soon afterward and seeing the fear behind their little eyes was heartbreaking. Despite the knowledge that we had always tried to empower our children throughout the many deployments with the idea that life goes on and we move forward when challenges arise, I wanted to be able to convey to them a more concrete sense of strength and hope that daddy's wounds would not stop the wonderful experiences we had enjoyed together and have planned for the future. It was especially important to me when I felt my resolve was not at full strength, wrestling with my own emotions. Reading a book at bedtime was our comfort and cuddle time, so a book seemed a great forum for this – something they could hold, see and go back to for reassurance during the harder moments, with someone or by themselves.

Through Tim's recovery we have been blessed to meet many other wounded families with an amazing resolve, although wrestling with similar issues. Their resilient children looked to the adults in their world to guide them through the enormous amount of unknowns about how their parent's injuries would affect them. Adults, like us, wanted to be able to offer their children comfort and found limited resources to help. When we adopted Cassidy at age 5 and three years into Tim's recovery, she too had questions about her daddy's "boo boos", especially as she experienced his second brain surgery and recovery. Our older children began expressing a desire to help her and

other children like them understand the hope and comfort they found. It was time to take those initial writings and develop them into something in which all families could find benefit. On behalf of all of us involved with this project, I hope you find the book to be a good resource and addition to your library.

Whether you are a parent, grandparent, family caregiver, friend, or teacher, as you read this book with those children looking to you for answers, please use it as a tool to empower not only their strength, but their creativity. Reassure them that they are not alone. There are many families around the nation experiencing these types of tragedies and yet find ways to live full and enjoyable lives together. Due to the severity of some individuals' injuries, the level of interaction between children and their parents compared to that depicted in the book may vary, however this book seeks to instill hope and acceptance so that in large or small ways, children can continue to find their wounded parent a part of their lives. Let them know they can help in the recovery and come up with new ways to have fun and be together. Encourage their questions and provide honest answers at a level for which you feel your children are ready. One of the hints our children relayed to us, was that it was scarier for them when they thought we were not telling them everything. They wanted and needed to know more information so we could put a name to it and talk about how to deal with it. The "not knowing" created more mystery and greater room for their imagination to create more gruesome images or worrisome thoughts. They appreciated the matter of fact way we presented Tim's traumatic brain injury and its side effects —what it was and what it meant, always ending on the positives and possibilities.

You are all stronger than you know! Believe in the invincibility of the inner spirit—yours and theirs!

—Shannon Maxwell

Author's Acknowledgements

This labor of love is absolutely a team effort. So many people influenced its creation and final presentation. I thank each and every one from the bottom of my heart. Together we have created a book that, I hope, will help children and their families find comfort and strength through recovery and life beyond.

Special gratitude:
To Liza Biggers, whose brilliant illustrations brought the book to life and captured the emotions of the situations— thank you for sharing your heart, your talent, and yourself.

To Tim, my husband and soulmate, who was, and continues to be, an inspiration to me and all those around him through his indomitable spirit and leadership—thank you for your support and love throughout this process.

To Alexis, Eric, and Cassidy, my beautiful, amazing children, who lived the story, gave their advice and input to the story, and live every day helping each other and those around them understand that Daddy's injuries do not stop life's enjoyment— thank you for your innocence, kindness and joy.

To Ethan Biggers who sacrificed his life for the freedoms of many and whose strength still lives on in his sister—thank you for your legacy.

To the Edmundson, Traub, Salau, Deathe/Sardinas, Moran, and Graham children and families who openly shared their stories to help other children find hope and happiness— thank you for your love and resilience.

To Mom, Dad, Ed and Lisa Kurdyla, Carole Turner, Heather Shannon, Maryruth Bracken, Annie Devlin, Jason Enterline, and Janelle Hill who believed in the book and helped guide it to print—thank you for your faith and for helping to make this book a reality.